EVERYBODY'S FAVORITE
CLASSICAL PIANO PIECES

W9-CXO-862

AMSCO PUBLICATIONS
NEW YORK/LONDON/PARIS/SYDNEY

Order no. AM1004597
International Standard Book Number: 978-1-4584-2314-6

Exclusive distributors:
Music Sales Corporation
257 Park Avenue South, New York, NY 10010 USA
Music Sales Limited
14-15 Berners Street, London W1T 3LJ, UK
Music Sales Pty. Limited
20 Resolution Drive,
Caringbah, NSW 2229, Australia

Contents Alphabetically by Composer

JOHANN SEBASTIAN BACH
Air On The G String from Suite No.3 In D Minor..........................8
Jesu, Joy Of Man's Desiring from Cantata 147....................5
Toccata And Fugue In D Minor....................10

LUDWIG VAN BEETHOVEN
Bagatelle In G Minor Op.119....................17
Sonata Pathétique Op.13 2nd movement....................20
Symphony No.7 Op 92 (Allegretto theme)....................25

ALEXANDER BORODIN
Nocturne from String Quartet No.2....................28

JOHANNES BRAHMS
Capriccio In G Minor from Fantasies Op.116, No.3....................34
Lullaby Op.49, No.4....................32

FRÉDÉRIC CHOPIN
'Fantasie-Impromptu' Impromptu No.4
    In C♯ Minor, Op.66 (Largo section)....................40
'Military Polonaise' Polonaise No.1 In A Major, Op.40....................43
'Raindrop Prélude' Prélude No.15 In D♭ Major, Op.28....................50
Prélude In E Minor Op.28, No.4....................48

CLAUDE DEBUSSY
Clair De Lune from *Suite Bergamasque*....................56
Golliwogg's Cakewalk from *Children's Corner*....................62

ANTONIN DVORÁK
Humoresque....................74

GABRIEL FAURÉ
Après Un Rêve Op.7, No.1....................68
Pavane Op.50....................71

EDVARD GRIEG
Piano Concerto In A Minor (Opening)....................76

GEORGE FRIDERIC HANDEL
The Arrival Of The Queen Of Sheba from *Solomon*....................86
The Harmonious Blacksmith, Air And Variations....................81
Zadok The Priest, Coronation Anthem....................90

FRANZ JOSEPH HAYDN
Serenade from String Quartet In F Major, Op.3, No.5....................94

SCOTT JOPLIN
The Entertainer....................99
Maple Leaf Rag....................104

FRANZ LISZT
Consolation No.3....................108

JULES MASSENET
Méditation from *Thaïs*....................138

FELIX MENDELSSOHN
O For The Wings Of A Dove from Psalm 55:
    'Hear My Prayer'....................113
Sweet Remembrance, No.1 from *Songs Without Words*
    Book 1, Op.19....................116

WOLFGANG AMADEUS MOZART
Piano Concerto No.21 In C Major (2nd movement)....................122
'Sonata Facile' Sonata In C Major, K545....................120

JACQUES OFFENBACH
The Can-Can from *Orpheus In The Underworld*....................140

MAURICE RAVEL
Pavane Pour Une Infante Défunte....................132
Piano Concerto In G (1st movement)....................129

ANTON RUBINSTEIN
Piano Concerto No.4, Op.70 (2nd movement)....................144

ERIK SATIE
Gnossienne No.1....................148
Gymnopédie No.1....................152

FRANZ SCHUBERT
Ave Maria....................156
Impromptu No.3 In B♭ Major, Op.142 (excerpt)....................158
'The Trout Quintet' Op.114 (4th movement)....................162

ROBERT SCHUMANN
Chiarina from *Carnaval*, Op.9....................166
The Wild Horseman from *Album For The Young*, Op.68....................169

PYOTR ILYICH TCHAIKOVSKY
June: Barcarolle, No.6 from *The Seasons*, Op.37....................178
Piano Concerto No.1 In B♭ Minor (Opening)....................184
Sentimental Waltz, No.6 from *Six Pieces*, Op.51....................171
Sweet Reverie, No.21 from *Album For The Young*, Op.39....................186

GEORG PHILIPP TELEMANN
Fantasia In B Minor....................189

Johann Sebastian Bach

born: 21 March 1685 in Eisenach, Germany

died: 28 July 1750 in Leipzig, Germany

Johann Sebastian Bach has come to be regarded as one of the geniuses of Western music, although during his lifetime many of his contemporaries achieved greater fame. His life was spent in a succession of posts as Organist and Director of Music in court or church establishments, composing whatever was required from him by his employers. Throughout his life Bach travelled all over Germany to hear other organists play. Through his travels and his extensive copying and arranging of other composers' work, Bach became familiar with the musical styles of Germany, Italy and France at that time. This legacy is seen in the breadth of compositional techniques he used, especially in his orchestral music.

In 1708 Bach took up the post of Court Organist at Weimar. During his time there he composed most of his huge output of works for the organ. In 1717 Bach applied to the court of Prince Leopold of Cöthen. With hardly any church services to compose for, most of Bach's compositions were for entertainment, in the form of orchestral and keyboard (harpsichord and clavichord) music.

The six *Brandenburg Concertos* (1721) and the beautiful *Concerto for Two Violins in D Minor* (1724) were written during his time at Cöthen, as were two of the four orchestral suites of which the 'Badinerie' from *Orchestral Suite No.2 in B Minor* and 'Air on the G String' from *Orchestral Suite No.3 in D Major* are justly famous. The first book of *The Well-Tempered Clavier* (1722) also written at this time, is a collection of 24 preludes and fugues written to celebrate the new 'well-tempered' tuning system, where all intervals on the keyboard are adjusted so that pieces in any major or minor key will sound acceptably in tune. Together with the second book (1740), the *'48'*, as the collection is known, is now part of the standard repertoire for any keyboard player.

In 1721 Bach married his second wife, Anna Magdalena. Together they had 13 children, in addition to the six he had with his first wife, Maria Barbara, who had died in 1720. In 1723 Bach landed the extremely prestigious job of Kantor of St. Thomas' Church in Leipzig. He had heavy responsibilities, involving providing music for four churches, training the choirs and teaching the organ. Among other things, he was required to compose a new cantata for choir, soloists and small orchestra each and every week.

A cantata consists of chorales (Lutheran hymns), choruses and arias, and are sung to meditate on the appropriate Biblical text for the time of year. The congregation would join in with the chorales and the chorale melody was often woven into the texture of the other movements to unify the work. The famous *Jesu, Joy of Man's Desiring* uses florid counter melodies written around the central chorale tune.

Bach composed around 300 cantatas in all, however, the foremost works of his Leipzig years must be his settings of the Passion story. A devout Lutheran all his life, Bach wrote several large-scale choral works for performance on Good Friday. They present the story of the Crucifixion through the most beautiful and heartfelt music.

As in the cantatas, the congregation would have joined the choir in singing the familiar chorale words and melodies. Of Bach's Passion settings, the *St. Matthew Passion* (1727) is pre-eminent. The narrator, a solo tenor, tells the story while the choir acts as the crowd and other soloists represent characters in the story.

In his later years Bach seemed to be setting down his lifetime's accumulation of compositional skill, often pursuing a musical idea or compositional technique to its full extent. He demonstrated his supreme mastery of fugal writing in *The Musical Offering* (1741) and *The Art of Fugue* (c.1745).

By the time he died in 1750 Bach was regarded by some as old-fashioned and was criticised for his complexity. Eternally inventive, thoroughly intellectual, and perhaps not fully appreciated in his day, Bach is now regarded as a supreme master of his art.

Jesu, Joy Of Man's Desiring

from Cantata 147

Composed by Johann Sebastian Bach

rall. poco a poco

Air On The G String

from Suite No.3 In D Minor

Composed by Johann Sebastian Bach

Toccata And Fugue In D Minor

Composed by Johann Sebastian Bach

14

Ludwig van Beethoven

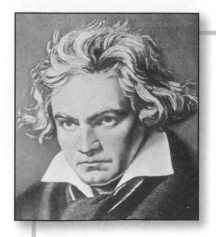

born: c.17 December 1770 in Bonn, Germany
died: 26 March 1827 in Vienna

Beethoven was born the son of a tenor chorister and a housemaid, who were both in service at the Court of the Elector of Bonn. The 'van' in the family's surname indicates that they were of Flemish origin, rather than connected to the aristocracy, although the composer was slow to correct misapprehensions on this point, and later in Vienna often spelt his own name 'von Beethoven'.

Beethoven's father was a boor and a bully who was determined, once his son had shown signs of musical talent, that the boy would outshine even the famous Mozart as a prodigy. Music was the only subject Ludwig was ever properly taught, although lessons were liable to begin in the middle of the night when his father returned drunk from the tavern and his pupil would have to be hauled from his bed. Despite the beatings, Beethoven's early concerts (including one infamous occasion where the 13-year-old performer was advertised as being only eight) were not successful.

In 1792 Beethoven went to Vienna to study, most notably with Joseph Haydn, and he stayed there for the rest of his life. As his fame as a pianist grew, demand for his compositions also increased. He was able to publish whatever he was inspired to write, for instance the lovely *Bagatelles*. Uniquely, he managed to survive in Vienna without being an employee of either the Church or the Court, but he did have wealthy patrons, such as Prince Carl von Lichnowsky, who supported him financially and put up with Beethoven's increasingly rude and eccentric behaviour. To the Prince, Beethoven dedicated his *Piano Sonata Op.13, 'Pathétique'*.

Beethoven took Classical forms and expanded them to heroic proportions undreamt of by Mozart and Haydn. His *Violin Concerto*, and his five piano concertos are all masterpieces of the genre. He also wrote music for many theatrical productions, including an overture for the play 'Egmont', by his friend, the poet Johann Wolfgang von Goethe. He was less successful in the realm of opera. His one attempt, *Fidelio*, cost him a great deal of effort and had to be rewritten many times. The *Overture* was in fact the fourth that Beethoven composed for the opera.

Beethoven is probably best known for his nine symphonies, which include *Symphony No.5*, with its famous 'fate knocking at the door' theme, and *Symphony No.6 'Pastoral'*, a wonderful description in music of a day out in the countryside.

Professional success for Beethoven was mirrored by private tragedy. By the turn of the 19th century he knew he was going deaf. In 1802 he wrote of his feelings of bitter despair in a heart-rending letter, known as the 'Heiligenstadt Testament', in which he struggled with thoughts of suicide. Astonishingly, he managed to continue to compose, and although his later works are often intensely personal and idiosyncratic they also include such life-affirming masterpieces as *Symphony No.7*, which Wagner later described as 'the apotheosis of the Dance'.

In 1817 Beethoven received a commission from the Philharmonic Society of London, for a symphony. When it was eventually delivered in 1824 they could hardly have expected a work on such a scale—*Symphony No.9 'Choral'*. The fourth movement calls for vocal soloists and a full choir in addition to the normal orchestra, as Beethoven here includes words for the first time in a symphony. It includes his setting of Schiller's *Ode To Joy*, which crowns this immortal work and has been used many times since as an anthem of peace and brotherhood. At the Viennese premiere, the composer, who had been following the music in the score, had to be turned round to face the audience at the end of the symphony as he could not hear the tumultuous applause.

In 1827 Beethoven died. His funeral route in Vienna was lined by thousands of mourners. This awkward, stubborn, angry man had changed the world of music forever.

Bagatelle In G Minor

Op.119

Composed by Ludwig van Beethoven

'Sonata Pathétique'

Op.13 (2nd movement)

Composed by Ludwig van Beethoven

24

Symphony No.7
Op.92 (Allegretto theme)

Composed by Ludwig van Beethoven

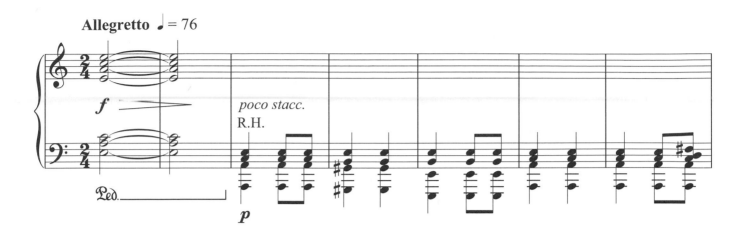

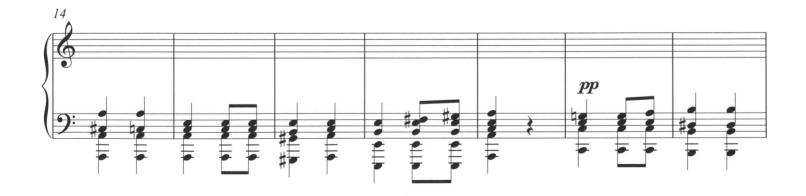

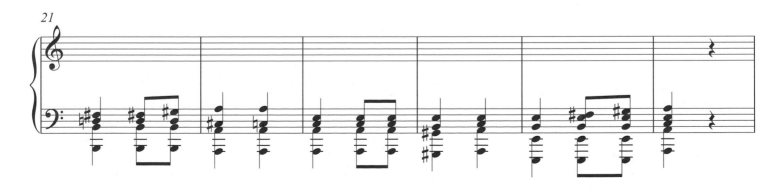

Nocturne
from String Quartet No.2

Composed by Alexander Borodin

29

Johannes Brahms

born: 7 May 1833 in Hamburg, Germany

died: 3 April 1897 in Vienna

Brahms was a Romantic composer who wrote beautiful, expressive music, full of passion and colour. His love of form and unity and use of eighteenth-century forms marked him out as a conservative rather than an innovator, and he was widely acclaimed in his day as the true upholder of the German Classical tradition.

Born into a modest family, from an early age he earned money by playing piano in taverns and arranging music for the light orchestra in which his father played the double bass. During this time he absorbed the irregular rhythms and melodic style of Hungarian gypsy music that featured in many of his own compositions. At the age of 15, Brahms gave his first solo piano recital. On tour in 1853 he met the violinist Joseph Joachim, who quickly became an important friend and influence. On the same tour, he met Robert Schumann and his wife Clara. Although Clara was 14 years Brahms' senior, he developed a romantic passion for her that lasted until she died.

Brahms' early works were mainly for piano, including three sonatas and his first piano concerto (in D minor). Despite his devotion to Clara, he nearly married Agathe von Siebold in 1858, who inspired a set of five songs composed in that year. Throughout his life Brahms favoured older forms (and in particular, variations), to give structure to his endlessly inventive explorations of simple ideas. In 1860 he signed a manifesto opposing the 'new music', placing himself publicly in the conservative camp, and was hailed by many as the true successor to Beethoven.

By 1863 Brahms had achieved some success as a pianist and published a lot of music, but he was eager for wider recognition. In search of a prestigious conducting post he moved to Vienna and became director of the Singakademie, a choral society with a tradition of singing unaccompanied music. He began to study and edit the music of earlier composers including Bach and Handel, and his admiration and scholarship of this music contributed to the 19th-century revival of Baroque music.

His most famous choral work, *A German Requiem*, was completed in 1868. The work is not a Latin mass for the dead, but a meditation on seven Biblical texts on death, mourning and comfort. Despite the acclaim the *Requiem* brought, Brahms fought shy of composing orchestral music until in 1874 he wrote the popular and attractive *Variations on St Anthony Chorale*. This, along with the *Requiem*, brought him international renown and financial security. Brahms now felt ready to write his four symphonies, each in the Classical four-movement format.

In 1878 Brahms composed his extremely difficult *Violin Concerto in D major* for his friend, Joseph Joachim. 1880 brought the popular Academic Festival Overture, written for Breslau University.

Since hearing Brahms' first symphony, the conductor and pianist Hans von Bülow had respected him as the upholder of tradition, and in 1881 he offered Brahms the use of the private Meiningen Orchestra, of which he was director. This encouraged Brahms further in his orchestral composition, and in 1881 he finished his second piano concerto (in B♭ major).

Throughout his life Brahms composed over 260 songs and a large amount of chamber music. He loved the simplicity of German folk-songs, like the *Lullaby*, but most of his songs are serious in tone and full of passion. Some of the finest examples of Romantic Lieder are to be found in the *'Magelone'* song-cycle, written in the company of Clara Schumann and her children.

Brahms' final achievements included his clarinet sonatas and the final sets of piano pieces. Over the years he wrote hundreds of heartfelt short piano pieces with titles such as 'Ballade', 'Intermezzo' and 'Capriccio', as well as more populist 'Waltzes' and 'Hungarian Dances'.

Brahms was hit hard by the deaths of his friends, especially Clara Schumann. Although only in his early 60s he contracted cancer of the liver in 1896 and died, artistically and financially successful, a year later.

Lullaby
Op.49, No.4

Composed by Johannes Brahms

dim. e rall. al fine

Capriccio In G Minor

from Fantasies, Op.116, No.3

Composed by Johannes Brahms

Frédéric Chopin

born: c.22 February 1810 in Żelazowa Wola, Poland

died: 17 October 1849 in Paris, France

Chopin was the son of a French émigré father and a cultured Polish mother. Displaying an early talent for the piano, he began his studies at the Polish Conservatory in 1826. In 1829 he made a concert tour, and while he was well received in Berlin and Vienna, the greatest acclaim came in his native Warsaw, where his use of Polish folk melodies and rhythms was particularly appreciated.

As a youngster of 19, Chopin was inspired to compose two piano concertos (*Op.11 in E minor* and *Op.21 in F Minor*) by his love for a singing student, Konstancja Gladkowska. The 'singing' quality of the piano parts is apparent throughout these works, particularly in the slow movements, and this melodic style is central to Chopin's view of composition.

Chopin settled permanently in Paris in 1831. He found patrons and became a sought-after performer and teacher in high society, where his good looks and impeccable social graces aided his popularity. Two extremes of piano playing and composition emerged at this time: one, championed by Franz Liszt, celebrated flamboyant showmanship and brilliant technical display, the other, represented by Chopin, had its roots in the private drawing room. Chopin composed intimate miniatures which, although requiring a flawless technique and sensitive colouring of the music, were not written to impress, but to express sentiments in an elegant manner.

The piano was the supreme Romantic instrument, reshaped, enlarged, and mechanically improved. Chopin exploited the instrument's new potential, devoting his entire composition career to it. His chromatic harmonies and remote modulations stretched the known harmonic language and he varied his treatment immensely, delaying or extending passages, introducing a greater complexity in the return of a theme, or adding a brilliant 'coda'.

His smaller-scale works, the études, préludes, nocturnes, polonaises, waltzes, impromptus and mazurkas, were probably written for teaching purposes, particularly the 27 études. These continued a tradition of pieces that used one musical idea to highlight a particular aspect of piano technique. Chopin transformed the étude from a mere teaching aid to a highly significant musical genre. Chopin's *24 Préludes* follow Bach's example of writing a set of pieces in every key. They include the famous *'Raindrop' Prélude*, in which the melody is underpinned throughout by a repeated A♭, suggesting the constant sound of rain.

Beautiful melodies are accompanied by delicate, often arpeggiated left-hand textures. The use of 'rubato' to create flexibility within the melody is very important to an effective performance. Chopin described this technique as a 'pushing forward' or 'holding back' of the right hand melody while the left hand always plays in strict time.

Chopin wrote his larger-scale works such as the scherzos, ballades and sonatas for his salon recitals. The Romantic sonata lost the formal structure which characterized Classical sonatas as composers experimented with form. These experiments with form resulted in pieces like the *Ballade in G Minor Op.23* and *Ballade in F Major Op.38*, which have a strong sense of drama and narrative drive.

In 1836 Chopin began an 11-year liaison, somewhat ambiguous in nature, with the novelist George Sand (real name Aurore Dudevant). She was a mother of two, separated from her husband, with striking looks and a reputation for intelligent, progressive thinking. In 1838 the couple went to the island of Majorca, but the damp conditions worsened Chopin's tuberculosis and they returned to France, staying in Sand's country home every summer until 1846. Sand was undoubtedly a huge inspiration to Chopin. His most deeply felt music comes from his years with her, and he wrote hardly anything after they parted. Without her nursing, Chopin's health quickly deteriorated and his professional life also began to falter.

In 1848 his sister began to care for him, until he finally succumbed to the tuberculosis that had dogged him throughout his life in October 1849, at only 39 years of age.

'Fantasie-Impromptu'

Impromptu No.4 In C♯ Minor, Op.66 (Largo section)

Composed by Frédéric Chopin

'Military Polonaise'

Polonaise No.1 In A Major, Op.40

Composed by Frédéric Chopin

45

Prélude In E Minor

Op.28, No.4

Composed by Frédéric Chopin

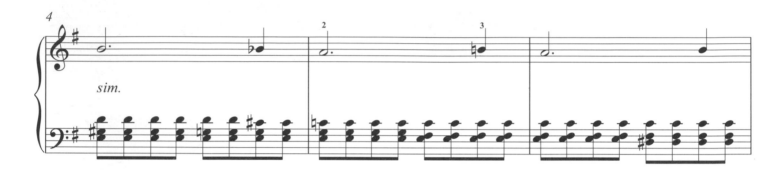

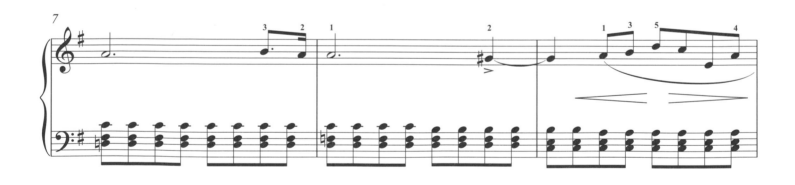

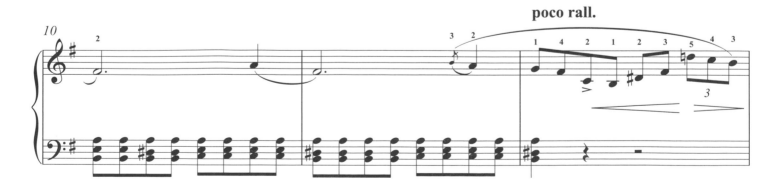

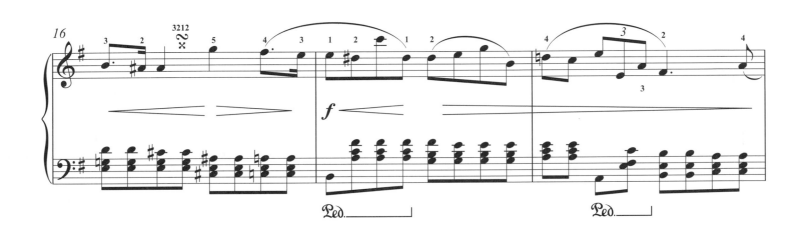

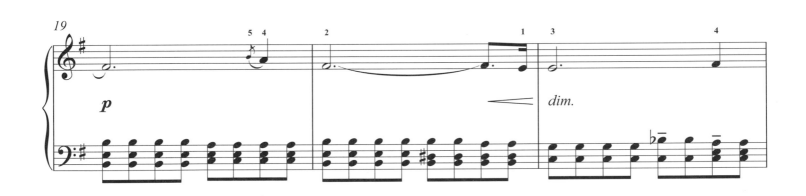

'Raindrop Prélude'

Prélude No.15 In D♭ Major, Op.28

Composed by Frédéric Chopin

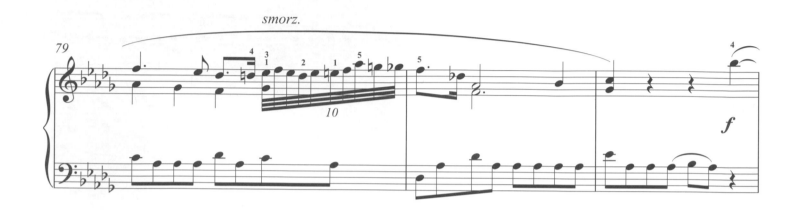

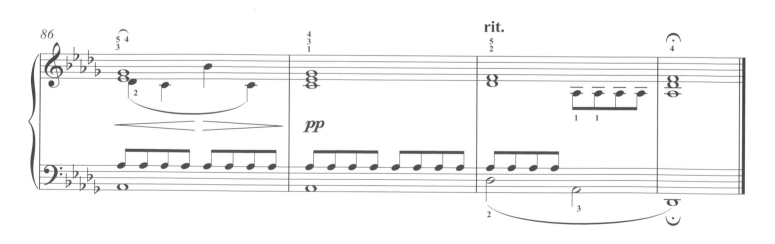

Claude Debussy

born: 22 August 1862 in Saint-Germain-en-Laye, France

died: 25 March 1918 in Paris

It was the exhibition in 1963 of Monet's painting 'Sunrise; An Impression' that ultimately gave birth to the term 'Impressionism'. Though it was a term Debussy did not like, it was suitable in that composers were obscuring the traditions of 'exhausted' harmony with new sonorities and colours, just as painters were obscuring the outlines of objects with gentle fogs and mists, or with the fuzzy reflection of street lights through an evening's drizzle of rain.

The symbolist poet Mellarmé said, "To name an object is to...sacrifice enjoyment...To suggest it—that is our dream." Perhaps this explains why, in the original score, the Piano Preludes' titles appear at the end of each piece, allowing an aural image to suggest itself before the identification of a scene, smell of a scent, or the invocation of a wonderful sound. *'Gardens In Rain'*, *'Reflections In The Water'*, *'Dead Leaves'*, *'Dialogue Of The Wind And The Sea'* are typical of the array of poetic titles to be found in his output.

Achille-Claude Debussy was the eldest of three brothers and a sister. His parents ran a little china shop before moving to Clichy and then to Rue Pigalle in Paris. Times were hard, and whilst his siblings were taken in by his aunt, he was left to his own education and could not attend school. His brother Eugene died of meningitis when seven years old, and Claude and his sister were taken to Cannes. In Cannes, he received piano lessons, and Mme Mauté de Fleurville (a former pupil of Chopin) pronounced that he should become a musician. Thus he entered the Paris Conservatoire aged 10, socially awkward and initially disliked.

He adored the music of Berlioz, Wagner, Mussorgsky and Lalo (once being escorted out of a theatre for being too enthusiastic) and abhorred Beethoven. In the summers of 1881 and 1882 he worked for Tchaikovsky's patron, Mme von Meck, in Russia. He failed to win the renowned Prix de Rome in 1883 but succeeded the following year and was to spend three years composing in the Villa Medici, meeting other artists such as Liszt, Verdi and Boito, but he found this a miserable experience and returned a year early. In 1894, he composed the tone-poem *Prélude à l'après-midi d'un faune* ('Prelude to the Afternoon of a Faun') based on Mellarmé's poem, which, along with his only string quartet, ensured much public discussion.

At the age of 40, his opera *Pelléas et Mélisande* offered confirmation that there was a composer changing musical history—the lyricism of his vocal writing and lack of movements made many feel the experience to be like one massive recitative. The writer, Maeterlinck, furiously and publicly wished it to be an "emphatic failure".

By many, Debussy was classed 'second rate' and unusual', but it took little time for his individuality to be indelibly established as the voice of a genius. He did not really care about the expected rules and formulae of the past as revealed when submitting a composition as a student. His tutor, Émile Rély, demanded, "Dissonant chords do not have to be resolved? What rules do you follow?" to which Debussy famously replied, "Mon plaisir!"

His use of large orchestral forces was not for sakes of power but for delicate employment of tone-colour, and subtle effects of motion and stillness. His overall 'impressionistic' sound perhaps comes from his use of the whole tone scale—sonorities that were unusually atmospheric and far removed from the mainstream harmony and the rich chromaticism of Wagner and Strauss. He turned away from the Classical era's rigid forms, and was drawn to a more refined offering of emotion than was present in the Romantic era before him. The piano music of Debussy was inspired by the younger Ravel's *Jeux d'eau* (1901) that offered a new realm of possibility into the world of technical skill and imaginative sound.

He said that he would write his memoirs in his 60s, but he developed cancer in 1910, was a near invalid by 1914, and died when he was 55, in 1918.

Clair De Lune

from *Suite Bergamasque*

Composed by Claude Debussy

Andante très expressif

Calmato

pp *morendo jusqu'à la fin*

Golliwogg's Cakewalk

from *Children's Corner*

Composed by Claude Debussy

Un peu moins vite

Cédez avec
un grande émotion

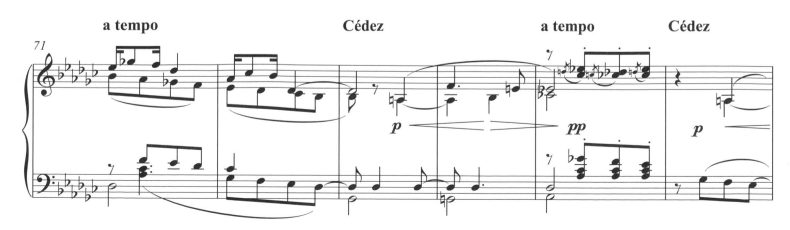

Gabriel Fauré

born: 12 May 1845 in Pamiers, France

died: 4 November 1924 in Paris

Fauré is often dismissed as a salon composer, best known for small forms such as songs and short piano pieces. However, he was the most advanced composer of his generation, writing music that was unmistakeably French but uniquely personal, especially in its use of harmony. His music embodies order and restraint, with clear texture and form.

Fauré was the youngest of six children. In 1854 he was sent to the École Niedermeyer in Paris, to train as a choirmaster and organist. One of his teachers was the composer Camille Saint-Saëns, who influenced him enormously. The training he received in the polyphonic music of the Renaissance era, plainsong and Church Modes (scales that are not major or minor but have different arrangements of tones and semitones) was crucial to his later style. He liked to create ambiguity between major and minor chords, and often flattened the leading-note in a key, creating a modal effect. Fauré was awarded the composition prize on leaving the École Niedermeyer in 1865, for his work Cantique de Jean Racine.

In 1871 Fauré formed the Société Nationale de Musique with fellow composers d'Indy, Lalo, Duparc and Chabrier, in order to champion French music. In 1874 he joined the music staff at the Madeleine church in Paris. In 1883 he married Marie Fremiet, with whom he had two sons. With a family to support Fauré needed to continue with the work he found tedious, namely his job at the Madeleine and teaching piano and harmony. There was little time for composing except in the summer holidays and he was extremely self-critical of his work and often depressed.

Nevertheless, Fauré's piano music from the 1880s is elegant and captivating. Influenced by Mendelssohn and Chopin, the music is lyrical rather than virtuosic. Fauré has been called the greatest master of French song, writing nearly 100 throughout his life. *Après un rêve* (1878) is Italian in style, while *Clair de lune* of 1887 was a setting of a poem by Verlaine, a poet whose work he set with great success, conveying atmosphere and feeling rather than specific images. During this period he also composed the enduringly popular *Pavane* (1887).

In the 1890s Fauré finally began to realise some of his ambitions. In 1896 he was promoted to chief organist at the Madeleine and succeeded Massenet as teacher of composition at the Paris Conservatoire of Music, where his pupils included Ravel. He finally achieved success with larger scale works, mostly incidental music for plays, and in 1900 he finished the orchestrated version of his *Requiem*, which he had begun composing in 1877. The work is a hauntingly beautiful setting of the Latin Requiem Mass, set for choir, organ and orchestra with soprano and baritone soloists. Fauré's characteristic unfolding of a melody is clearly heard, making much use of one or two melodic and rhythmic ideas. The lines are spun out with an inevitability and sense of direction that is not interrupted by his sudden key changes and often ambiguous harmony.

In 1905 Fauré became director of the Paris Conservatoire and finally achieved fame and recognition. The latter period of his life was his most productive, despite deafness and distortion that affected his perception of the highest and lowest sounds. His compositions gained more expressive force, with bold harmony.

In 1920 Fauré retired from the Conservatoire a celebrity and was finally free to concentrate on composition. He was awarded the Grand Croix of the Légion d'Honneur, an unprecedented honour for a musician, and was much admired by younger French composers.

In his last years he concentrated on composing some extremely fine chamber music. He was in poor health for the last two years of his life and died in Paris on 4th November 1924. He had linked the end of the Romantic era in France with the 'modern' style emerging in the twentieth century, and remained the most technically advanced French composer until Debussy.

Après Un Rêve

Op.7, No.1

Composed by Gabriel Fauré

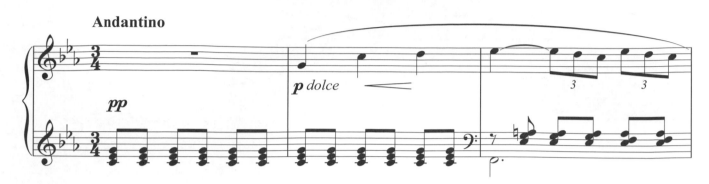

70

Pavane

Op.50

Composed by Gabriel Fauré

Humoresque

Composed by Antonin Dvořák

Piano Concerto In A Minor

(Opening)

Composed by Edvard Grieg

George Frideric Handel

born: 23 February 1685 in Halle, Germany

died: 14 April 1759 in London

Handel was one of the great composers of the Baroque era. A truly cosmopolitan figure, he was born in the town of Halle in Saxony, but spent most of his life in England. The British truly appreciated his music and his most famous works were written for them.

Handel had music lessons with Zachow, the organist at the Church of Our Lady in Halle. In 1703, after a short spell at Halle Cathedral, Handel moved to Hamburg, the principal centre of German opera, and composed his first opera, *Almira*, there. From 1706 to 1710 Handel lived in Italy. These were very important years for Handel as he laid the foundations of his compositional style.

In 1710 Handel returned to Germany to become the Director of Music at the Electoral Court of Hanover. He soon left to visit London for a year where he had another operatic triumph with *Rinaldo*. Handel returned to Germany but was back in London in 1712, having been granted leave 'for a reasonable time'. However, he was still there two years later when his master, the Elector of Hanover, was crowned King George I of England!

Handel settled into a long and prosperous career in London, patronised by the royal family and held in high regard by the British public. At the same time, Handel was engaged to compose operas and find singers for the Royal Academy of Music, a company set up to present Italian opera to the London public. Handel composed many of his 41 operas, including *Giulio Cesare* and *Rodelinda* for performance at the King's Theatre, Haymarket, and later at the Covent Garden Theatre.

In 1729 the Academy collapsed and Handel took over the theatre as entrepreneur as well as composer. More operas followed, including *Alcina* and *Xerxes*, but times were changing. A rival company, The Opera of the Nobility, was set up in 1733 and the two companies battled for singers, composers and audiences. With the bankruptcy of both opera companies in 1737, Handel took a new direction. He turned his attention to the oratorio, a dramatic idiom for soloists and chorus, usually based on an Old Testament story, which was essentially an opera but performed in concert rather than staged. Handel was writing for a new audience, the expanding British middle classes, who were much happier listening to Biblical tales.

Handel expanded the role of the chorus in his oratorios, using the British choral tradition to advantage. Little-used in his operas, the chorus became essential to the dramatic impact of the oratorio. In the mid-1730s Handel leased a theatre for oratorio performances during Lent, when opera was not permitted. The concerts were extremely popular and had the added bonus of a performance, from Handel himself, of his own organ concertos during the interval. In 1741 he travelled to Dublin to give a series of concerts for charity, the visit culminating in the first performance of *Messiah*, the most famous choral work in the English-speaking world. Handel's genius at writing for the chorus is exemplified in *Messiah*, from which comes the famous and dramatic 'Hallelujah' Chorus. At a performance of *Messiah* in London the King was so moved by this chorus that he stood up, a tradition that has remained ever since.

Some of the instrumental music from the oratorios became well-known pieces in their own right, for example, *The Arrival Of The Queen Of Sheba*, which is the overture from the oratorio *Solomon*. Such was the popular appeal of his music, Handel was often commissioned to compose for state events. His four anthems for the Coronation of George II in 1727 included *Zadok The Priest*, which has been sung at every British coronation since.

Handel's eyesight began to fail as he finished his last oratorio Jephtha and by 1753 he was virtually blind. He died in 1759 at the age of 74. Very much a 'national institution', the esteem in which London music lovers held Handel was demonstrated at his funeral and burial in Westminster Abbey, which was attended by 3000 of his loyal public.

The Harmonious Blacksmith

Air And Variations

Composed by George Frideric Handel

Var. 3

The Arrival Of The Queen Of Sheba

from *Solomon*

Composed by George Frideric Handel

Zadok The Priest

Coronation Anthem

Composed by George Frideric Handel

Andante maestoso

Franz Joseph Haydn

born: 31 March 1732 in Rohra, Austria
died: 31 May 1809 in Vienna

Haydn's family history offers no clues to the huge fame he would achieve during his lifetime as one of the master composers of the Classical Era. He was born into a family of wheelwrights in an Austrian village on the Hungarian border. His roots lay in Hungary, although there is reason to believe that the family had origins in Croatia, which accounts for the Slavonic element in his music.

By the age of eight, Franz Joseph had obtained a place in the choir school of St. Stephen's Cathedral in Vienna, where he served as one of the principal soloists and received tuition in harpsichord, violin and organ. At eighteen, and no longer much use as a choirboy, Haydn was dismissed and supported himself through teaching, playing the organ in church services and performing in orchestras and string quartets. He began composing, taking early influence from the powerful 'Sturm and Drang' style of C. P. E. Bach's sonatas.

The turning point of his career came in 1761 when he was appointed to a position in the household of the Esterházys, one of the wealthiest and most influential families in Austria. In 1776 his position was elevated to Kapellmeister (or music director). With the support of a discerning patron (the Esterházy prince, Prince Nikolaus I), an excellent orchestra and creative freedom, Haydn flourished — "I could, as head of an orchestra, make experiments, observe what created an impression, and what weakened it, thus improving...and running risks. I was set apart from the world...and so I had to become original."

Works from these early years include around 125 trios, various early comic operas, and nearly 400 courtly dances. His early string quartets (one of which includes the *Serenade*) provided attractive court entertainment, but also displayed maturity in their freshness and deceptive simplicity as Haydn moved away from the stately Baroque and ornamented Rococo styles. This elevation of music from mere entertainment into more original forms is also manifest in his early symphonies, and allowed him to adopt a more serious character in line with German and Austrian trends.

In 1779 Haydn was granted a new contract which allowed him to compose works for other patrons and publish his work. With this newfound freedom, Haydn received commissions from further afield — he wrote a series of Parisian symphonies (1785–86) and was commissioned to write *The Seven Last Words* for Holy Week in Cadiz Cathedral. Haydn was well received in England also, visiting London on two occasions (1791–92 and 1794–95), conducting weekly concerts and premiering new works. His last 12 symphonies were all composed for these trips, including the *Surprise Symphony*, *Military Symphony*, *Drumroll Symphony* and *London Symphony*, along with the *Oxford Symphony*, performed when he was awarded an honorary Doctorate of Music from Oxford University.

Back in Vienna, Haydn resumed work for the Esterházys, and his compositions from this period include six masses and his two oratorios, *The Seasons* and *The Creation* (his biggest choral masterpiece, inspired by having heard Handel in London). He also continued to write quartets, including the *Emperor*, but he was to write no more symphonies.

Haydn spent the last years of his life in retirement surrounded by the love of friends and the respect of younger musicians. In May 1809, when Napoleon's armies invaded Vienna, Bonaparte himself ordered a guard to be placed outside the composer's home where he lay on his deathbed.

In terms of his vocal works, Haydn heralds the close of an epoch rather the dawn of a new one, while in his instrumental music (particularly in his string quartets and symphonies), he is granted the unrivalled position of first great master.

He emancipated melody from its confinement to ceremonial courtliness and, infusing it with his native folk music, gave it vitality. Above all, Haydn wrote with directness, simplicity and humour, the following remark he once made about himself being the most revealing: "Anyone can see that I'm a good-natured fellow".

Serenade

from String Quartet In F Major, Op.3, No.5

Composed by Franz Joseph Haydn

Andante cantabile

Scott Joplin

born: c.1867 in Texarhana, Texas

died: 1 April 1917 in New York City

Joplin was central to the creation of ragtime, a heady mix of syncopation and catchy melody. Initially seen as 'black music' from the red-light areas and Vaudeville shows, it gradually gained respectability across America and reached Europe in 1900 when the band-leader Sousa, Joplin's white counterpart in American popular music, took arrangements of ragtime to Paris. Debussy and Stravinsky experimented with it in their piano music, and even Brahms intended to write a rag before he died.

Ragtime was a fusion of white marches and Western harmony with folk music and black rhythms from African drumming. In a piano rag the right hand plays off-beat melodies with a fluctuating sense of meter. This effect was difficult to master, and one early ragtime pianist called it "playing two different times at once". The influence of Sousa is found in the left hand, which imitates the 'oom-pah' bass-line of the march, providing a solid foundation for the syncopation above. The form of a rag mirrors the march, typically having four or five themes in two or more keys. Although ragtime was written to dance to, it is known from early piano rolls and recordings that rubato and exaggerated speed changes were an accepted part of its performance.

Joplin was one of six children of an ex-slave father and a free mother. He was given free music lessons in his hometown then left home, aged 14, and became an itinerant musician moving from town to town to find work. After working in St.Louis and Chicago he settled in Sedalia, Missouri in 1896. A quiet, thoughtful man, Joplin began to change attitudes among the 'respectable' classes towards ragtime. The 'sinful' syncopated music didn't seem so bad when played by this modest man.

Gradually ragtime became popular with white people, which brought money and the chance for Joplin to publish his *Original Rags* in 1899. In that same year, publisher John Stark heard Joplin play at the Maple Leaf Club in Sedalia. Stark published the *Maple Leaf Rag* and with his financial backing it brought fame for Joplin, selling over a million copies across America.

Stark, Joplin and his new wife Belle all moved back to St.Louis in 1901. *The Peacherine Rag* and *The Easy Winners* were written in 1901, followed by *Elite Syncopations* and *The Entertainer* in 1902. Joplin tried to capture the sound of the tremolo style of the mandolin in *The Entertainer*.

Relations between Joplin and Stark became strained as Joplin, against Stark's advice, wanted to try his hand at larger forms. He immersed himself in writing an opera, *The Guest of Honor*, which was only performed once in 1903. The score was then lost and its whereabouts remain unknown.

After an unsettled few years which included a split from his first wife and the death of the second, Freddie Alexander, Joplin settled again in New York in 1907. He met and married his third wife Lottie Stokes, and in 1908 he published *Pine Apple Rag* and *Fig Leaf Rag* as well as the instruction manual *The School of Ragtime*. Despite the success of *Solace* and the *Paragon Rag* (in 1909), ragtime was in trouble. Stark's business was in decline as other styles overshadowed ragtime. Joplin and Stark finally went their separate ways and Joplin submerged himself in opera, this time with the three-act *Treemonisha*.

Treemonisha dominated Joplin's last years. He began to suffer mood swings, and although he staged one performance of the opera in 1916, he had no costumes, props, nor even a proper theatre. *Treemonisha* flopped, and Joplin was crushed. His wife finally had him committed to an asylum and he died a broken man in 1917.

Joplin's music remained largely ignored until the 1970s ragtime revival, which included a successful production of *Treemonisha* on Broadway and the use of *The Entertainer* in the film 'The Sting'. Shamefully neglected in his lifetime, Joplin now stands as a creative genius who left a unique legacy of a truly American popular style.

The Entertainer

Composed by Scott Joplin

(repeat R.H. 8va. higher)

Maple Leaf Rag

Composed by Scott Joplin

Consolation No.3

Composed by Franz Liszt

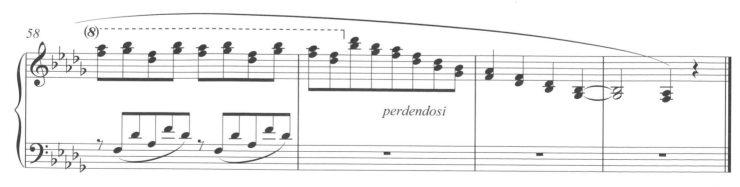

O For The Wings Of A Dove

from *Psalm 55: 'Hear My Prayer'*

Composed by Felix Mendelssohn

Sweet Remembrance

No.1 from *Songs Without Words Book 1*, Op.19

Composed by Felix Mendelssohn

Wolfgang Amadeus Mozart

born: 27 January 1756 in Salzburg, Austria

died: 5 December 1791 in Vienna

Although Mozart lived a short life, he became one of the most influential and highly respected composers and performers of all time. His sister, Maria 'Nannerl' Anna was also a brilliant musician and his father Leopold was a talented court musician, composer and violin teacher. Even as a toddler, Mozart was picking out tunes by ear and by 1761 was composing his own pieces. His father recognised these rare gifts and promptly took his children on a series of grand tours, displaying their prodigious talents to the rest of the world. After trips to places such as Vienna and Munich in 1762, Paris in 1763, London in 1764 and Holland in 1766, Mozart finally returned to Salzburg in 1766, having already written many compositions including the *Minuet in F Major* (K2).

Mozart's output from 1769–77 increased at an incredible rate, and he produced nearly 300 compositions, including the *Piano Sonata No.5 in G* (K283) and over 20 symphonies. During this time he also managed to tour Italy, where he was honoured with a knighthood in Rome.

On 9th July 1772, Mozart was formally employed as Konzertmeister at the Salzburg Court, a position that had previously been unpaid. Mozart was frustrated at his attempts to leave Salzburg, but eventually managed to embark on a trip with his mother late in 1777, visiting Mannheim and Paris. Here, amongst other things, he composed the variations on *'Ah! Vous Dirais-Je Maman'*, the theme of which is better known as the nursery rhyme 'Twinkle, Twinkle, Little Star'. Mozart's mother Anna Maria became ill and died in Paris in 1778. Mozart then travelled on to Munich alone, returning to Salzburg in 1779.

In 1782 he married Contanze Weber in St. Stephen's Cathedral, having decided to settle permanently in Vienna. The Mozarts finally visited Salzburg again in the summer of 1783. It is during this summer holiday that he probably wrote several piano sonatas for Nannerl, including the *Piano Sonata in A* (K331) with its brash 'Rondo Alla Turca'.

In 1783, the Mozarts had their first child, Raimund Leopold, but he died after only two months. They went on to have a further five children, three of whom died in infancy. Despite these sorrowful events, Mozart's first years in Vienna were musically and financially very successful. This was largely because of Mozart's subscription concert series', in which he played and conducted his own pieces such as the piano concertos in *D minor* (K466) and *C major* (K467), which is also known as 'Elvira Madigan' after the film in which the piece features.

Mozart was also well known among his musical colleagues, often holding soirees and playing chamber music with them. They included the great composer Haydn, who is reported to have said to Leopold Mozart, 'Before God, I tell you that your son is the greatest composer known to me in person or by reputation'.

In 1786 Mozart wrote the opera *The Marriage of Figaro* (K.492), and was the toast of both Vienna and Prague. Following this success he prepared a further collaboration with his preferred librettist, Lorenzo Da Ponte, on the subject of Don Juan—*Don Giovanni* (K.527) was premiered in Prague in October 1787. Mozart's father had died earlier that year in Salzburg, and it must have seemed as if the final link to his birthplace had been severed.

Having moved to cheaper lodgings in the suburbs in the summer of 1788, Mozart found fresh inspiration and composed his final three symphonies. Despite Mozart's deepening financial crisis, there seems to have been no reward or commission for this mammoth task—it appears that he composed them solely for his own gratification.

Although he was still experiencing modest success in Vienna, Mozart was far from financially stable. In his final year, Mozart seemed to go into overdrive, working on three operas (including *The Magic Flute* K.620), the *Clarinet Concerto in A* (K.622) and the *Requiem* (K626), which remained unfinished at his death in 1791.

'Sonata Facile'

Sonata In C Major, K545

Composed by Wolfgang Amadeus Mozart

Piano Concerto No.21 In C Major

(2nd movement)

Composed by Wolfgang Amadeus Mozart

Piano Concerto In G

(1st movement)

Composed by Maurice Ravel

Pavane Pour Une Infante Défunte

Composed by Maurice Ravel

1er Mouvt. Très lointain

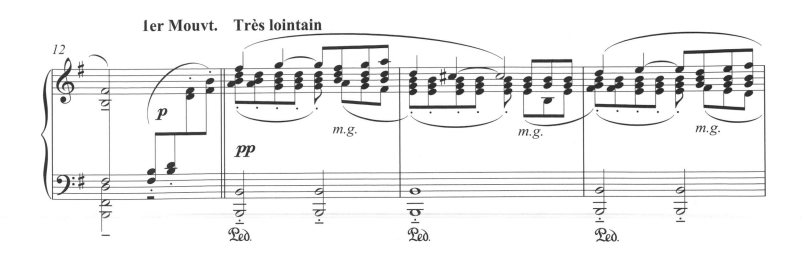

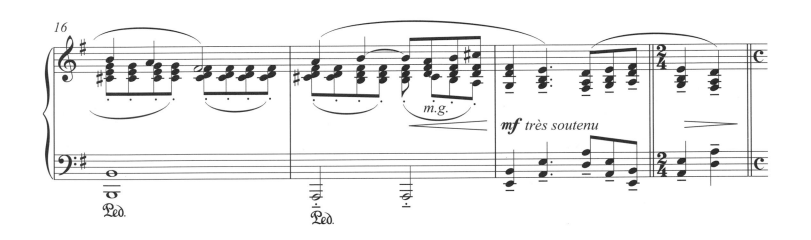

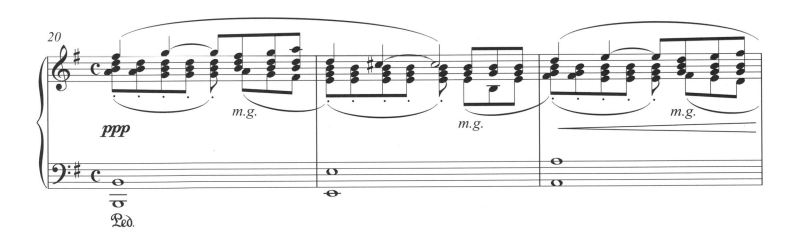

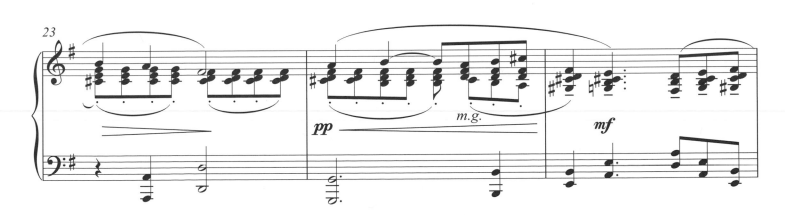

1er Mouvement
marquez le chant

Très grave

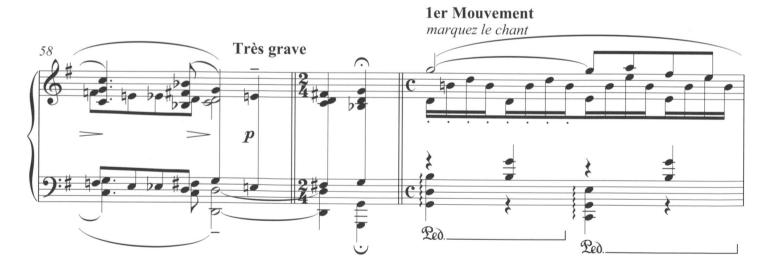

Cédez

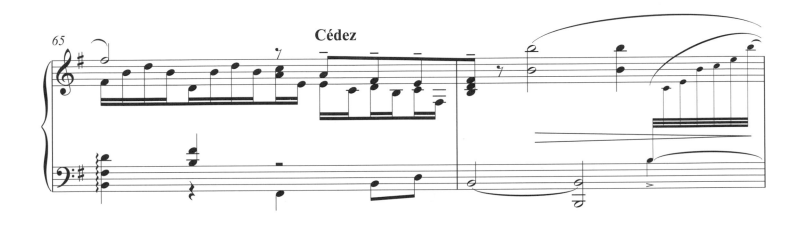

Reprenez le mouvement

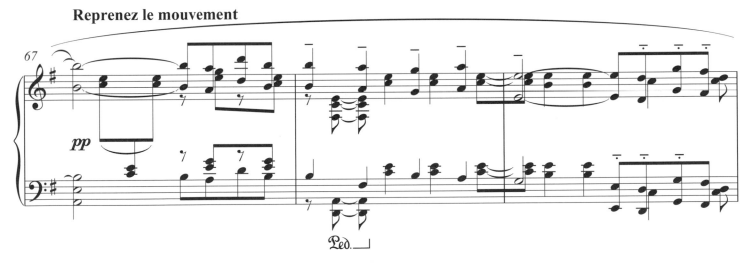

En élargissant beaucoup

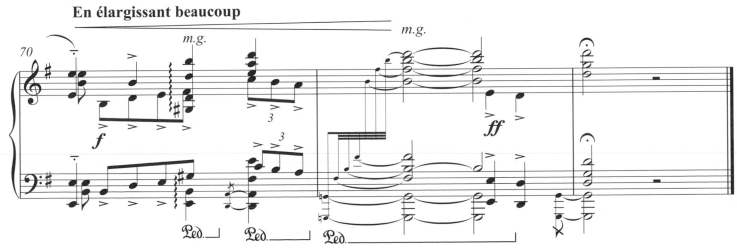

Méditation

from *Thaïs*

Composed by Jules Massenet

rall.   a tempo

The Can-Can

from *Orpheus In The Underworld*

Composed by Jacques Offenbach

Piano Concerto No.4

Op.70 (2nd movement)

Composed by Anton Rubinstein

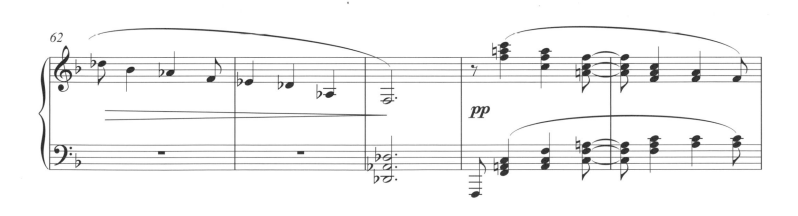

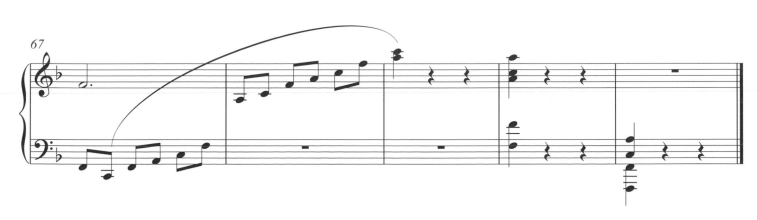

Gnoissienne No.1

Composed by Erik Satie

Lent

Très luisant (Shining)

Questionnez (Questionning)

Du bout de la pensée (From the tip of the thought)

Postulez en vous-même (Wonder about yourself)

Pas à Pas (Step by step)

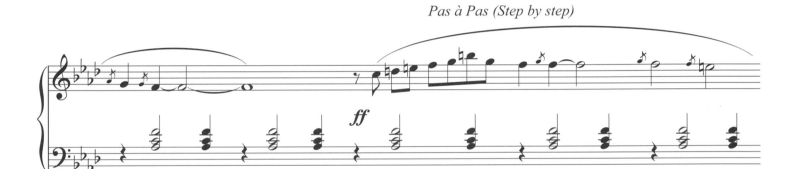

Sur la langue (On the tip of the tongue)

Gymnopédie No.1

Composed by Erik Satie

Lent et douloureux

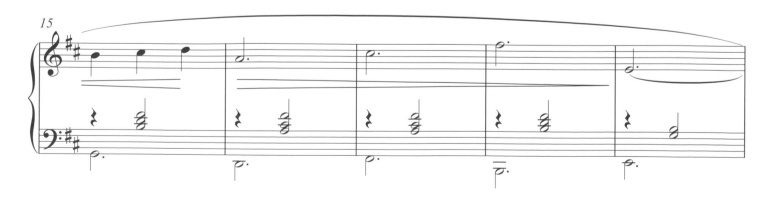

Franz Schubert

born: 31 January 1797 in Vienna
died: 19 November 1828 in Vienna

Schubert was born in the city where Haydn, Mozart and Beethoven rose to greatness before him. Like Mozart, Schubert was a man of prodigious musical talent and prolific output whose life was tragically short and beset with financial difficulties and disappointments. Although only 31 when he died, Schubert displayed a maturity and depth of emotion in his music that many composers who lived much longer never achieved.

In 1813, having been taught piano and violin by his brother and his father, Schubert began to train as a teacher. During training he composed three symphonies, three masses, chamber music, nearly 150 Lieder (German songs), four short operas and many short piano pieces. Schubert has been called a 'Romantic Classicist' since he faithfully used forms and harmonic language from the Classical tradition of Mozart and Haydn. He composed nine symphonies, 22 piano sonatas, 35 chamber works, six masses and 17 operas, all in recognisable Classical forms. But his greatest legacy is the 600 Lieder, which exquisitely embody the poems he set (often on Romantic themes such as nature, the supernatural and love) using beautiful melodies and richly inventive piano accompaniments.

Schubert was a very private man who rarely performed in public, preferring to premiere compositions at musical evenings in private drawing-rooms, or 'Schubertiads' as these gatherings became known. He gradually acquired a wide circle of like-minded, musically literate acquaintances and friends who championed his music. Schubert's supreme gift was his ability to write sublimely beautiful melodies that embody a whole range of emotions, from deep melancholy to great joy. This melodic gift is evident in all of Schubert's compositions, but is distilled in his Lieder.

Although his greatest outpouring of Lieder was between 1813 and 1818, he wrote songs throughout his life. Schubert re-used his immensely popular song *The Trout* with its vivid depiction of the bubbling brook and the darting fish as the fourth movement (a set of variations) of his lively piano quintet of 1818. By this time his musical circle had grown to include poets, dramatists, painters and singers, and he finally had some songs published after a long period of indifference from publishers.

Schubert wrote nine symphonies in all—the early ones are rarely heard nowadays, but the fourth, fifth, eighth and ninth remain popular, though the eighth (1822) remained unfinished. The two movements that comprise the work are full of mystery and pathos, with dark sinister melodies played on hushed lower strings. Perhaps this reflects his state of mind, as in 1822 Schubert contracted syphilis.

After 1822 Schubert returned to his family home after many happy years lodging with friends. He was very ill and his song-cycle the *Fair Maid of the Mill* (1823) contains a lot of poetry on themes of despair and resignation—typical Romantic themes, but surely reflecting his personal state. On a lighter note, he wrote incidental music for the play *Rosamunde* that year. The play sank into obscurity but Schubert's incidental music remained popular.

By 1825 the Schubertiads, which had dwindled somewhat, came to prominence again. Although by now very ill, Schubert composed his large-scale ninth symphony (although he never heard it performed) and more piano music was published. He wrote extensively for the piano, including 22 sonatas, but his many shorter piano pieces or 'miniatures' contain some of his best-known music. Schubert composed the eight Impromptus and the six *Moments Musicaux* in 1827, and these pieces are to the piano what the Lied was to the voice. Each evokes a particular mood and demonstrates different aspects of writing for the piano, providing a benchmark for subsequent composers.

In 1828 Schubert finally gave a public concert for the Vienna Philharmonic Society. He continued to compose, including the masterpieces that are the *String Quintet in C* and his final *Piano Sonata in B-flat*. These include some of Schubert's darkest music. He died on 19th November, and his gravestone bears the epitaph 'The Art of Music here entombs a rich possession but even finer hopes.'

Ave Maria

Composed by Franz Schubert

Moderato

157

Impromptu No.3 In B♭ Major

Op.142 (excerpt)

Composed by Franz Schubert

VAR. II.

'The Trout Quintet'

Op.114 (4th movement)

Composed by Franz Schubert

Chiarina

from *Carnaval*, Op.9

Composed by Robert Schumann

168

The Wild Horseman

from *Album For The Young*, Op.68

Composed by Robert Schumann

Pyotr Ilyich Tchaikovsky

born: 7 May 1840 in Votkinsk, Russia

died: 6 November 1893 in St. Petersburg

Tchaikovsky was undoubtedly the greatest Russian musical talent of the Romantic era. With his gift for eloquent melody and his mastery of writing for the orchestra he created dramatic and evocative works through which he could express something of his tortured private life.

He showed early promise at the piano and began to compose seriously after his mother died in 1854, but he was obliged to take a job in the Ministry of Justice after he left school. However, in 1863 he entered the St. Petersburg Conservatory.

Although Tchaikovsky championed traditional Russian music and culture, his musical education at the Conservatory was entrenched in the Western Classical tradition, a legacy he passed on when he became Professor of Harmony at the Moscow Conservatory in 1866. Because of this, Tchaikovsky stood apart from his 'nationalist' contemporaries who were concerned with developing a particularly Russian style.

'The Five', as they were known, heavily criticised Tchaikovsky's *First Symphony*. However, the leader of the group, Mily Balakirev, encouraged him by suggesting he write a work based on Shakespeare's 'Romeo and Juliet'. Balakirev gave Tchaikovsky a plan for the work and even wrote the first four bars. The result was the *Romeo And Juliet Fantasy Overture* (1869), which remains a popular concert piece. The most famous work of this early period is his *Piano Concerto No.1 in B minor* (1874–75).

In 1876 Tchaikovsky began a 14-year correspondence with a wealthy widow, Nadezhda von Meck. She supported him emotionally and financially on the condition that they should never meet. She became his confidante as he struggled with his homosexuality and his desire to avoid public shame. To 'cure' himself, he married Antonina Miliukova in July 1877. She had professed her love for him in a letter just three months earlier. The marriage was a shambles and by October the couple were permanently separated. Tchaikovsky's near-hysterical state is recorded in letters to Mme von Meck and his brother Modest, as well as being clearly apparent in his music. *Symphony No.4* is full of emotional excess and hysteria, and the opera *Eugene Onegin* has obvious parallels to his own situation, as it tells the story of a girl who is rejected by a man who fascinates her.

Although known primarily as an orchestral composer, Tchaikovsky wrote over 100 pieces for the piano. *The Seasons*, a suite of 12 piano pieces, was published throughout 1875–76 in a monthly periodical. Two years later he composed the *Album For The Young*, a set of 24 pieces with descriptive titles, which he declared to be '…in the style of Schumann'.

After a long stay in Europe, Tchaikovsky returned to Russia in 1878 and soon after he resigned from the Moscow Conservatory and lived on his allowance from Mme von Meck. The strain of trying to obtain a divorce affected his work, his wife only finally agreeing to it when she had an illegitimate child. However, during this period he wrote what was to become one of his most famous works, the *1812 Overture*. Commissioned to celebrate the 70th anniversary of Russia's victory over Napoleon in 1812, Tchaikovsky did not have much enthusiasm for the piece and declared it to be 'very loud and noisy', but it was an immediate success and its popularity has never waned.

The anguished and sorrowful *Symphony No.6*, first performed on October 28th 1893, was given the title 'Pathétique' by Tchaikovsky's brother Modest. Three days after the premiere, Tchaikovsky was brought before a court of his peers from his old school. He was accused of bringing the school into disrepute through rumours of his homosexuality and was sentenced to commit suicide.

One week later, Tchaikovsky was dead. The cause of his death is shrouded in uncertainty. The official reason given was that he died from cholera as a result of drinking untreated water, but it is also possible that he killed himself by taking arsenic.

Sentimental Waltz

No.6 from *Six Pieces*, Op.51

Composed by Pyotr Ilyich Tchaikovsky

June: Barcarolle

No.6 from *The Seasons*, Op.37

Composed by Pyotr Ilyich Tchaikovsky

Piano Concerto No.1 In B♭ Minor

(Opening)

Composed by Pyotr Ilyich Tchaikovsky

Sweet Reverie

No.21 from *Album For The Young*, Op.39

Composed by Pyotr Ilyich Tchaikovsky

Fantasia In B Minor

Composed by Georg Philipp Telemann

Con pompa

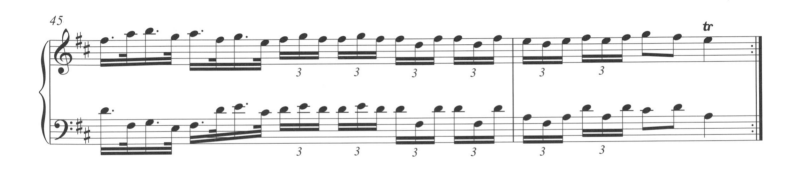

D.C. al Fine